Anna Cora Mowatt

Fashion

Adapted and Abriged as a One-Act

by Aurand Harris

Single copies of plays are sold for reading purposes only. The copying or duplicating of a play, or any part of play, by hand or by any other process, is an infringement of the copyright. Such infringement will be vigorously prosecuted.

Baker's Plays
c/o Samuel French, Inc.
45 West 25 Street
New York, NY 10010
bakersplays.com

NOTICE

This book is offered for sale at the price quoted only on the understanding that, if any additional copies of the whole or any part are necessary for its production, such additional copies will be purchased. The attention of all purchasers is directed to the following: this work is fully protected under the copyright laws of the United States of America, the British Commonwealth, including Canada, and all other countries of the Copyright Union. Violations of the Copyright Law are punishable by fine or imprisonment, or both. The copying or duplication of this work or any part of this work, by hand or by any process, is an infringement of the copyright and will be vigorously prosecuted.

This play may not be produced by amateurs or professionals for public or private performance without first submitting application for performing rights. Licensing fees are due on all performances whether for charity or gain, or whether admission is charged or not. Since performance of this play without the payment of the licensing fee renders anybody participating liable to severe penalties imposed by the law, anybody acting in this play should be sure, before doing so, that the licensing fee has been paid. Professional rights, reading rights, radio broadcasting, television and all mechanical rights, etc. are strictly reserved. Application for performing rights should be made directly to BAKER'S PLAYS.

No one shall commit or authorize any act or omission by which the copyright of, or the right to copyright, this play may be impaired. No one shall make any changes in this play for the purpose of production.

Publication of this play does not imply availability for performance. Both amateurs and professionals considering a production are strongly advised in their own interest to apply to Baker's Plays for written permission before starting rehearsals, advertising, or booking a theatre.

Whenever the play is produced, the author's name must be carried in all publicity, advertising and programs. Also, the following notice must appear on all printed programs, "Produced by special arrangement with Baker's Plays."

Licensing fees for FASHION are based on a per performance rate and payable one week in advance of the production.

Please consult the Baker's Plays website at www.bakersplays.com or our current print catalogue for up to date licensing fee information.

Copyright © 1981 by Aurand Harris
Made in U.S.A.
All rights reserved.

FASHION
ISBN **978-0-87440-874-4**
#1073-B

CAST

ADAM TRUEMAN, *a Farmer from Catteraugus*
COUNT JOLIMAITRE, *a fashionable European Importation*
COLONEL HOWARD, *an Officer in the U.S. Army*
MR. TIFFANY, *a New York Merchant*
SNOBSON, *a rare species of Confidential Clerk*
MRS. TIFFANY, *a Lady who imagines herself fashionable*
SERAPHINA TIFFANY, *her daughter, a Belle*
GERTRUDE, *a Governess*
MILLINETTE, *a French Lady's Maid*

SCENE: *New York City*
TIME: *1850*

FASHION

SETTING: *A splendid Drawing Room in the house of Mrs. Tiffany. Down Left is a large doorway leading to the main hall and stairs. Down Left is a door leading to the music room. At the back is a large archway leading to the conservatory, which is bright with flowers and sunlight. There are two small doors, one Up Right and one Up Left.* MILLINETTE, *a French Maid, is arranging some pillows. She sings a lively French Song.*

MILLINETTE. *Parfait!* (*Looks about the room*) Ah, de room *ressemble* exactly like de great *salones de Paris*. Madame Tiffany vill be *tres* proud of Millinette. (*Confidentually to audience*) I tell you in *confidence* Madame Tiffany is a lady of fashion. Monsieur make de money. Madam spend it. Monsieur nobody at all. Madame everybody altogether. Ah! De money is all dat is *necessaire* in dis country to make one lady of fashion. I teach Madame de latest *les modes de Paris*, and Madame set de fashion for all New York.

MRS. TIFFANY. (*Off*) Millinette!

MILLINETTE. *Oui*, Madame.

MRS. TIFFANY. (*Enters D.L., dressed in the most extravagant height of fashion*) Is everything in order, Millinette? Ah! Very elegant, very elegant indeed! There is a *jenny-says-quoi* look about the room. Is there not, Millinette?

MILLINETTE. Oh, *oui*, Madame!

MRS. TIFFANY. Miss Seraphina is not dressed yet? Oh, but I remember that is nothing more fashionable than to keep people waiting. Is it not so, Millinette?

MILLINETTE. *Oui*, Great *personnes* always do make little *personnes* wait.

MRS. TIFFANY. (*Aside*) This girl is worth her weight in gold. Millinette, how do you say "arm-chair" in French?

MILLINETTE. *Fauteuil.*

MRS. TIFFANY. Fo—tool! How refined. Fow-tool! Armchair! What a difference. Like hat—so common. Chapeau—so elegant. Tell Seraphina to hurry.

MILLINETTE. *Oui*, Madame.

MRS. TIFFANY. (*Talks to herself in the mirror, thinking she is alone*) I remember when I worked as a milliner, sewing and tying ribbons on hats—

MILLINETTE. Madame, sewing?

MRS. TIFFANY. (*Startled*) I mean—when I visited a millinery shop, TRYING on chapeaux, I—Oh, do tell Seraphina to come immediately!

MILLINETTE. I sink she *raide. Oui*. She *arrive*. (*She curtsies and exits D.L. after SERAPHINA enters D.L. Seraphina, too, is very extravagantly dressed*)

MRS. TIFFANY. My dear, how bewitchingly you look. Does Millinette say that that head dress is strickly Parisian?

SERAPHINA. Oh, yes, Mama, all the rage!

MRS. TIFFANY. Count Jolimaitre will soon be here. He is the most fashionable foreigner in town. Being accustomed to only nobility abroad, he can hardly tolerate the vulgarity of Americans. But I noticed he was quite attentive to you at Mrs. Proudacre's ball. So, my dear, you may devote yourself to him. Yes, he would be quite eligible as a husband for a daughter of the Upper Ten Thousand! (*Bell rings*) Oh, he is here! A-dolph will let him in. Good gracious! I am so flurried, and nothing is so ungenteel as agitation. He's coming up! Smooth your dress. Stand by the *faw-tool.*

SERAPHINA. Stand where?

MRS. TIFFANY. By the *faw-tool! Faw-tool!*

COUNT. (*Enters D.L., very dashingly dressed*) Madam.

MRS. TIFFANY. *Entray, sol vous pliat.* Oh, Count, this unexpected honor—(*Curtsies*)

FASHION

SERAPHINA. Oh, Count, this inexpressible pleasure—

COUNT. (*Bows to each*) Beg you won't mention it, Madam. Miss Seraphina, your most devoted. Ah, I find there is one redeeming charm in America—the superlative loveliness of the feminine population. (*Aside*) And the wealth of their obliging papas.

MRS. TIFFANY. My dear Count, I am sure you are at home in all the courts of Europe.

COUNT. Courts? Oh, yes, Madam. I am known in many courts in Europe. (*Aside*) Including a few POLICE COURTS. But I find very little refinement, very little *elegance* outside of Paris. Why at the last dinner I attended in England, given by Lord—Lord Knowswho, would you believe it, Madam, there was one present who wore a black cravat and took SOUP TWICE.

MRS. TIFFANY. Oh, Count, *im-pos-ee-ble*!

SERAPHINA. America, then, has no charm for you?

COUNT. There are some exceptions. I find you, for instance, particularly *charmante*. Your smile transports me to the summit of Olympus.

SERAPHINA. Then I must frown, for I would not send you so far away. (*Bell rings*)

MRS. TIFFANY. The bell! Who? *Excusay*. (*Calls D.L.*) A-dolph, announce—I am NOT AT HOME.

COUNT. In a word, Madam, I was tired of civilized life and I had *le desire* to refresh myself in a barbarous country, so I came to New York.

TRUEMAN. (*Off*) Out of my way! Don't tell me I can't come in. Can't you see? I am in!

MRS. TIFFANY. Who can it be? So *vul-gaire*!

TRUEMAN. (*Off*) I've come to see my old friend, Antony Tiffany.

MRS. TIFFANY. (*Aside*) One of my husband's plebeian acquaintances. What shall I do?

TRUEMAN. (*Enters D.L. dressed as a farmer, a stout cane in hand*) Where is she? Where is this woman that's not AT HOME in her own house?

MRS. TIFFANY. Sir, how dare you intrude yourself into my parlor?

TRUEMAN. Oh, you're the one.

MRS. TIFFANY. I am Mrs. Tiffany.

TRUEMAN. Anthony's wife, eh? Well, I'll shake on that.

MRS. TIFFANY. Sir, it is not the fashion in Paris to shake hands.

TRUEMAN. (*Aside*) Poor woman, she doesn't know what country she's in. Madam, I've known your husband since he was a little lad. His father was my best friend. I watched little Antony grow up. A young peddler he was, carrying his goods on his back.

MRS. TIFFANY. (*Aside*) What will the Count think? Sir, without doubt, you are speaking of someone else.

TRUEMAN. No. Antony Tiffany. Now I hear he's grown rich, and of course grown older—like me and you.

MRS. TIFFANY. Sir, a woman of fashion never grows old.

TRUEMAN. Eh?

MRS. TIFFANY. Age is always out of fashion. Now I will say, good day, Sir.

TRUEMAN. I thought city folks had better manners. I expected a civil welcome, or I wouldn't have come all the way from Catteraugus for a visit with you and yours.

MRS. TIFFANY. A visit!

TRUEMAN. Yes, I've come to see my old friend, Antony. (*Aside*) And to see what's happened to young Gertrude. I hope she's not that dressed-up critter. I don't believe, Madam, you've introduced me to the young lady?

MRS. TIFFANY. It is not the fashion in Paris, Sir, to introduce.

TRUEMAN. Thunder and lightning, woman! This is America.

MRS. TIFFANY. (*Aside*) How shall I get rid of him? Count Jolimaitre, please *par-doan* the errors of this rustic.

COUNT. (*Inspecting Trueman through his eye-glass*) Pray, Madam, is it one of the aboriginal inhabitants of the soil? To what tribe of Indians does he belong? Does he carry a tomahawk?

TRUEMAN. Something quite as useful—do you see that? (*Shakes stick*)

MRS. TIFFANY. Oh, dear! I shall faint. Millinette! Millinette!

MILLINETTE. (*Enters D.L.*) *Oui*, Madame.

MRS. TIFFANY. A glass of water. *Toot-de-sweet*! (*Rising to her full dignity*) Sir, the gentleman to whom you speak is *tres distinguished*. He is a Count. (*MILLINETTE looks at Count, starts and screams. COUNT, after a short surprise, plays with his eye-glass, and looks perfectly unconcerned*) What is the matter? What is the matter?

MILLINETTE. Noting, noting—only—(*Looks at Count and turns away*) only—noting at all.

TRUEMAN. Don't be afraid, girl. Did you never see a live Count before? He's tame—I dare say your mistress there leads him about by his ears.

MRS. TIFFANY. This is too much! Millinette, send for Mr. Tiffany instantly.

MILLINETTE. He *arrive* now, before, dis *moment*. (*Curtsies and Exits D.L.*)

TRUEMAN. My old friend! Where is he? I long to see his friendly smile.

MRS. TIFFANY. Count, *voo-ley-oo a-com-po-nay* Seraphina and *moi* into the *con-sir-va-twire*. (*COUNT bows and takes Seraphina's arm*) Pray walk this way, *sal vous plait*. (*They Exit at back*)

TRUEMAN. *Sal vous plait*. Ha, ha, ha! She's so fashionable she's forgot how to speak her mother's tongue. (*Turns to doorway D.L.*) Where are you Antony? (*Aside*) We'll see what fashion has done for him.

MR. TIFFANY. (*Enters D.L., followed by SNOBSON, his clerk*) My old friend! Adam Trueman! (*To Snobson, who Exits D.L.*) Wait for me in the hall. (*Shakes hands formally*) We are happy to welcome you, Sir, happy that you are our guest.

TRUEMAN. Happy? I'm not so sure. Your fine lady of a wife greeted me with the message SHE WAS NOT AT HOME. Refused to shake my hand. It's not the fashion, she says. And now I look at you—and see your face is crissed crossed with worried frowns. I'm afraid it's many a day since you were HAPPY at anything.

MR. TIFFANY. True, my work is heavy.

10 FASHION

TRUEMAN. See me, man! Seventy-two last August! Live a simple country life. Strong as a hickory and every whit as sound!

MR. TIFFANY. I take the greatest pleasure in remarking your superiority, Sir.

TRUEMAN. Bah! No man takes a pleasure in the superiority of another! Why the deuce can't you speak the truth? But I suppose it's—not the fashion. (*SNOBSON enter D.L. and stands by doorway*) Come, cheer up. I'd rather see one of your old smiles, than know you had made another thousand dollars. Your business is sound, I hope? Nothing rotten at the core? (*SNOBSON coughs*)

MR. TIFFANY. Yes, solvent; but the fact is, you can be of some assistance to me.

TRUEMAN. That's the FACT is it? I'm glad we've hit upon one TRUTH. (*SNOBSON coughs louder*) Who's that puppy barking at his fleas?

MR. TIFFANY. My confidential clerk.

TRUEMAN. Confidential? I wouldn't trust him with my spittoon.

SNOBSON. Sir, a word with you, if you please.

MR. TIFFANY. Speak on, Mr. Snobson, I attend.

SNOBSON. What I have to say, Sir, is an HONEST matter of importance to the CREDIT of the concern, Mr. Tiffany.

MR. TIFFANY. Oh, yes. (*To Trueman*) Excuse me for a moment. Urgent business.

TRUEMAN. (*Aside*) From the looks of that one—UNDERHANDED business.

MR. TIFFANY. If you will please make yourself comfortable in the library. This way, Sir. (*Goes to door U.L.*)

TRUEMAN. (*Aside*) I'll be more comfortable after I see young Gertrude. I worry. Will she, also, be bitten by the FASHION bug? (*Goes U.L.*) Thank you, Antony. I can do with a bit of a rest. (*Exits U.L.*)

MR. TIFFANY. I will be with you soon. (*Shuts door*) Now, Mr. Snobson, proceed.

SNOBSON. My salary, Mr. Tiffany.

FASHION

MR. TIFFANY. It has been raised three times within the last year.

SNOBSON. Still it is insufficient for the necessities of an honest man—mark me, an HONEST man, Mr. Tiffany.

MR. TIFFANY. (*Aside*) Will I never be rid of his blackmail? Very well, another hundred shall be added.

SNOBSON. There is one other subject which I have before mentioned, Mr. Tiffany—your daughter.

MR. TIFFANY. (*Aside*) Villian! Only the hand of my daughter will seal his lips. Very well, Sir. It shall be as you desire.

SNOBSON. And Mrs. Tiffany shall be informed that I'm to be THE MAN?

MR. TIFFANY. Yes. I'll to her at once.

SNOBSON. Enough said! That's the ticket! The CREDIT of the concern is safe, Sir.

MR. TIFFANY (*Aside*) How low have I bowed to this insolent rascal! Unless I can shake him, he will surely crush me! (*Exits at back*)

SNOBSON. And now I'll find Miss Seraphina and state my case. The old woman needn't try to knock me down now with any of her French lingo! Six months from today if I ain't driving my own tandem down Broadway—and as fashionable as Mrs. Tiffany herself, then I ain't the trump I thought I was! (*Looks at watch*) Bless me! Half past and I haven't had my julep yet! Snobson, I'm ashamed of you! (*He Exits D.L. GERTRUDE enters U.R., humming a popular song. She is a young girl, simply but becomingly dressed. She sees no one is about, goes to conservatory entrance. As she picks a rose, COLONEL HOWARD Enters D.L. He is a handsome young army man, dressed in uniform. He sees her and comes to her quickly*)

HOWARD. Miss Gertrude.

GERTRUDE. Colonel Howard!

HOWARD. It is quite fitting that I find you among the roses.

GERTRUDE. I enjoy tending the flowers. They remind me of the country.

HOWARD. I'm afraid you live a sad life here in the city. You came from a pleasant little town.

GERTRUDE. Geneva.

HOWARD. And were surrounded by kind friends. Here you are imprisoned by the frigid world of fashion.

GERTRUDE. Oh, it is true, I prefer a ramble in the woods to a promenade in Broadway. Ah, I see I have shocked you. You think I, being so "unfashionable," that I am totally without taste.

HOWARD. No. I, too, like a simple life. And I admire you—and your truthfulness.

GERTRUDE. I have no reason to conceal the truth. I was brought up, an orphan, by two kind sisters in Geneva. I had abilities, and desired to use them. I came here and am employed to teach music to Miss Seraphina. You see, I have my independence.

HOWARD. I—admire your spirit, Gertrude. I admire—

GERTRUDE. Colonel Howard, I must remind you that Mrs. Tiffany only receives visitors on her reception day. (*TRUEMAN enters U.L., stops, listens, and remains unseen*)

HOWARD. Nay, Gertrude, it is not Mrs. Tiffany, nor Miss Tiffany, whom I came to see. It—it is—(*Aside*) If I only dared to give utterance to what is hovering upon my lips.

GERTRUDE. Yes, Colonel Howard?

HOWARD. Gertrude, I must—must—

GERTRUDE. Yes, indeed, you MUST, must leave me!

HOWARD. Your book—(*Starts to give her book*)

GERTRUDE. Mrs. Tiffany would not be pleased to find you here. And we should not be found alone. Pray, pray leave me. (*She hurries him out D.L.*) What a strange being is man! Why should he hesitate to say—nay, why should I prevent his saying, what I would most delight to hear? Truly man IS strange—but woman is quite as incomprehensible!

TRUEMAN. (*Aside*) It is Gertrude. Yes, there is a light in her face—the same light that was in another face, which I remember so well.

GERTRUDE. Sir?

TRUEMAN. You are Gertrude?

GERTRUDE. Yes.

TRUEMAN. I am an old friend of Mr. Tiffany, from Catteraugus.

GERTRUDE. Mr. Trueman! Yes, Mr. Tiffany has spoken of you. I am glad to meet you, Sir. I, too, come from the country. Geneva.

TRUEMAN. Ah, Geneva. The Wilson sisters?

GERTRUDE. You are acquainted with them?

TRUEMAN. I shouldn't wonder if I was.

GERTRUDE. Then we have much to talk about!

TRUEMAN. (*Aside*) Ah, much more than she knows. I hear that you have no mother?

GERTRUDE. No, Sir. I wish I had.

TRUEMAN. (*Aside*) So do I! Heaven knows, so do I! And you have no father?

GERTRUDE. No, Sir, I often wish I had.

TRUEMAN. Don't do that, girl. Wish you had your mother, but never wish that you had a father again! Perhaps the one you had did not deserve such a girl.

GERTRUDE. (*Listens*) Mrs. Tiffany! They are coming in from the conservatory.

TRUEMAN. Thunder and Lightning! Right when we were getting acquainted.

GERTRUDE. I must prepare for Miss Seraphina's lesson. Oh, Mr. Trueman, I feel already we are friends. Thank you for coming! (*Goes U.R.*)

TRUEMAN. No, don't thank me.

GERTRUDE. Very well. You may not let me thank you, but you cannot prevent my feeling of happiness. (*Exits U.R.*)

TRUEMAN. (*Looking after her*) If falsehood harbours there, I'll give up searching after truth!

MRS. TIFFANY. (*Off*) Your stinginess will ruin me, Mr. Tiffany. (*TRUEMAN looks toward back, then quickly, comically, hurries out D.L., as MRS. TIFFANY, followed by MR. TIFFANY, Enters at back*) You must know that to be fashionable it is necessary to KEEP UP APPEARANCES.

MR. TIFFANY. It was for FASHION'S sake that you insisted upon this expensive house. It was for FASHION'S sake that you ran me in debt. It was for

FASHION'S sake, Madam, that I am on the very brink of bankruptcy!

MRS. TIFFANY. So much the greater reason that nobody should suspect. Only last week Mrs. Honeywood—

MR. TIFFANY. Gave a ball the night before her husband shot himself. Perhaps you wish to drive me to follow his example?

MRS. TIFFANY. Good gracious, no! Mr. Tiffany, how you talk! I consider black the most unbecoming color.

MR. TIFFANY. And while I have your ear, Madam—I have decided on the man who will marry Seraphina.

MRS. TIFFANY. The Count, of course.

MR. TIFFANY. No, that I will not permit.

MRS. TIFFANY. Mr. Tiffany, you are out of your senses!

MR. TIFFANY. That would not be very wonderful, considering how many years I have been united to you, my dear. Modern physicians pronounce lunacy infectious!

MRS. TIFFANY. And whom do you wish our daughter to marry?

MR. TIFFANY. Mr. Snobson.

MRS. TIFFANY. A clerk!

MR. TIFFANY. Have I not told you that I am in the power of this man! He is calling today. (*Looks off L.*) Ah, indeed, he is here now.

SNOBSON. (*Enters D.L.*) How dye do, Marm. How are you?

MRS. TIFFANY. *Bung jure.*

SNOBSON. Ah, to be sure—very good of you—fine day.

MRS. TIFFANY. (*Aside*) What ignorance.

SNOBSON. How is Seraphina?

MRS. TIFFANY. Miss Tiffany is not visible this afternoon.

SNOBSON. Not visible? I suppose that's the English for can't see her. Mr. Tiffany, Sir—what am I to understand by this de-fal-ca-tion, Sir?

MR. TIFFANY. Have patience, Mr. Snobson. All has been arranged.

SNOBSON. No humbug? All correct, eh? Well, Marm, don't make a stranger of me. If you've got any odd jobs about the house to do up, I shan't miss you. Seraphina and I'll get along very cosily by ourselves.

MRS. TIFFANY. Permit me to inform you that in France a mother never leaves her daughter alone with a young man.

SNOBSON. But, Marm, we ain't in France. (*Aside*) The woman thinks she's somewhere else than where she is.

MRS. TIFFANY. Now if you will *excusay moi*, it is time for Seraphina and I to take our afternoon ride in the park.

SNOBSON. Righto! I'll be glad to keep you company.

MRS. TIFFANY. Our *tete-a-tete* is at an end, Mr. Snobson. I wish you *bon swear*. (*Exits D.L.*)

SOBSON. Swear! Mr. Tiffany, am I to be fobbed off by a *bon swear*? Damn it, I will swear!

MR. TIFFANY. Patience, Mr. Snobson.

SNOBSON. An HONEST man keeps his word.

MR. TIFFANY. Your engagement to Seraphina will be announced. Now I must see if Mr. Trueman's quarters are ready. (*Exits D.L.*)

SNOBSON. I brought the old boy to his bearings, didn't I? Say the word, HONEST, and he jumps. I'll just have another mint julep, and drink a toast to my engagement to be! And Mrs. Tiffany, I say to you, *bon swear* that! (*Exits D.L.*)

SERAPHINA. (*She and the COUNT enter at back*) We must not tarry so long. Mama will be worried. No one here.

COUNT. Then we are alone—again. (*Clock chimes*)

SERAPHINA. Two o'clock. Time for our afternoon drive. It's all the rage! You must ride with us in our carriage.

COUNT. Ah, there's no resisting you, Miss Tiffany.

MILLINETTE. (*Enters with wrap*) Mademeiselle, I bring dis scarf for de ride. Keep you cozy in de breeze.

SERAPHINA. You are certain the scarf is the latest fashion?

MILLINETTE. (*Gives Count a threatening look, arranges scarf over Seraphina's shoulders, turns her around so she is facing the other way*) Mademoiselle, *permettes-moi.* (*Aside to Count*) Traitor! If Mademoiselle vill stand *tranquille* one *petit moment*. (*Aside to Count*) I must speak vid you!

COUNT. Sh!

MILLINETTE. I tell all.

COUNT. Sh. We will talk later.

MILLINETTE. (*Nods*) Ve vill return here.

COUNT. No.

MILLINETTE. I tell all!

COUNT. Yes! Return here.

SERAPHINA. What is that you say, Millinette?

MILLINETTE. Dis scarf make you so very beautiful, Madomiselle. *Tres parisienne!* (*Whispers to Count*) Ve meet here. (*He nods. She curtsies to Seraphina and exits D.R.*)

COUNT. (*Aside*) Not a moment to lose! Or—I am exposed! Miss Tiffany, I have an unpleasant piece of intelligence. You see, I have just received a letter from the—aw—Earl of Airshire; the truth is, the Earl's daughter has distinguished me by a tender *penchant*.

SERAPHINA. And they wish you to return and marry the young lady. But surely you will not leave us, Count?

COUNT. If YOU bid me stay, I couldn't AFFORD to tear myself away. (*Aside*) I'm sure that's honest. Say the right word—say that you will be my Countess—

SERAPHINA. Oh, you must not think of leaving. I—yes—yes, Count, I do consent.

COUNT. (*Aside*) I thought she would. (*Embraces her*) Enchanted, rapture, bliss, ecstasy, and all that sort of thing—words can't express it. But our wedding must be kept a secret. And our nuptials must take place in private. We will elope. Sh! (*Whispers*) Now.

SERAPHINA. (*Whispers*) Elope?

COUNT. It is the latest fashion. (*She nods*) Hurry. Pack some things. We will get the carriage—before your mother does. Ah, we part—but only for a moment—my petite bird of paradise.

SERAPHINA. I fly! (*Exits D.L.*)

COUNT. Ah, if only I were not so irrestible! But I find handling two women at once is TOO much. The only course of valor is—to be off! (*He starts D.L., freezes when he hears Millinette*)

MILLINETTE. (*Enters D.R., whispers*) Gustave... We be all of us alone?

COUNT. Ah, Millinette, my *cherie*, you see I am here as you bid.

MILLINETTE. Vat for you leave me in Paris? Vat for you leave me—and I love you so much? Ven you sick—you almost die—did I not stay by you—take care of you? Vat for you leave Paris?

COUNT. I was forced by uncontrollable circumstances.

MILLINETTE. Vat you do vid all de money I give you? The last *sous* I had—did I not give you?

COUNT. I dare say you did, *ma petite*. (*Aside*) And I wish you'd been better supplied. (*GERTRUDE enters U.R., unpreceived*) But we must not talk here. I will explain everything later.

MILLINETTE. No! You not deceive me no more.

SERAPHINA. (*Off*) Millinette? Millinette!

COUNT. Go. I will meet you—

MILLINETTE. Ven? Vere?

COUNT. In the music room. (*Points D.R.*) Alone... in five minutes. I will explain it all, my sweet, *adorable*, Millinette.

MILLINETTE. I vill be dere. You be, also. And you give me one grand *explanation*!

SERAPHINA. (*Off*) Millinette!

MILLINETTE. *Oui*, I come. Five minutes. Or I vill tell all. (*Exits D.L.*)

COUNT. Haste is the word. Hold the carriage at the side door. Appease Millinette. And marry Seraphina. (*Exits D.L.*)

GERTRUDE. (*Advancing from hiding*) Meet in the music room. Explain—what? This man is an impostor! If I tell Mrs. Tiffany—No, she will disbelieve me. To convince Seraphina would be equally difficult, and this rashness may render her miserable for life. No. She shall be saved! *I* must devise some plan for opening their eyes. (*Has an idea*) Ah, if I could expose the Count... if I could learn the truth from his own words.

18 FASHION

Yes, Seraphina is sure to detain Millinette. Meantime, I will hide myself in the music room, pull the draperies, disguise my voice, use my best French, and unmask this insolent pretender. But this is impudence—if I should fail? Fail! To lack courage when faced with difficulty is not a woman's failing. (*She Exits into music room, D.R. as COLONEL HOWARD enters D.L.*)

HOWARD. Miss Gertrude—Gertrude, I—(*She has gone. He is left holding the book*) In my haste I forgot—your book. (*Aside*) I—I will speak. I will ask her hand in marriage. Gertrude, I have returned to ask you—(*He looks into the room, Aside*) Whatever is she doing? Darkening the room—closing the window curtains. I wonder what...? But it is without honor to spy. Yet—(*He looks again. The door swings shut*) And now the door is shut. Footsteps. I must not be caught eavesdropping. (*He hides*)

COUNT. (*Enters, D.L., cautiously*) Caution is the word. Ah, the door is shut. She is there. (*Tiptoes to door. Knocks*) Open, my *petite cherie*. (*Door opens*) Where are you? I cannot see you in the dark.

GERTRUDE. (*Off, imitating Millinette's voice*) Hush. *Parle bas.*

COUNT. (*Enters doorway*) Come and give me a kiss! (*Door shuts behind him*)

HOWARD. (*Steps out from hiding, speaks aside*) A kiss! Oh, Gertrude! (*Hides again*)

MILLINETTE. (*Enters D.L.*) Now I vill know de truth. I vill make one grand discovery! (*Opens door D.R.*) *Mon Dieu!* Vat do not I see?

COUNT. (*Off*) Millinette! Out there! Who is this in here?

MILLINETTE. Ma'mselle Gertrude! Vat you do? Together! In de dark! I vill scream! (*She screams, looks at door, screams again, gasps for breath, and again screams and cries*)

MRS. TIFFANY. (*Enters D.L., followed by TRUEMAN*) What is the noise? How dare you create this disturbance in my house?

MILLINETTE. Look! You vill not believe. See! In de dark. Together!

MRS. TIFFANY. Who? (*COUNT enters*) The Count! (*GERTRUDE enters*)

TRUEMAN. Gertrude!

MILLINETTE. Oh, I not feel vell! My poor heart—broken a *million* pieces. You traitor! You villian! You—Oh, I go—I die of de broken heart. (*Exits D.L.*)

MRS. TIFFANY. (*To Gertrude*) What is the meaning of this?

TRUEMAN. (*To Count*) You scroundel! I'll beat the truth out of you, if there's any in you. (*Raises stick*)

COUNT. (*Rushes to Mrs. Tiffany*) Madam—my dear Madam—keep off that barbarous old man, and I will explain! I am perfectly innocent in this affair. (*Aside*) And that's the truth. When I entered that room, Madam, I—I did not know SHE was there. 'Pon my honor! Miss Gertrude, say if that is true or not true.

GERTRUDE. Sir, you know that you planned to meet—

COUNT. Answer a simple yea or nay. Did I know YOU were in that room?

GERTRUDE. I will be truthful. No, he did not know *I* was there, but he—

COUNT. You hear, Madam, I am innocent!

MRS. TIFFANY. Then YOU, you shameless girl, you planned it!

TRUEMAN. I won't believe it.

HOWARD. (*Steps forward from hiding*) It is true.

MRS. TIFFANY. Colonel Howard!

HOWARD. Would that I could tear out my tongue, but honor is at stake. She drew the curtains. She arranged —the rendezvous. Oh, Gertrude, I have striven to find some excuse—but this is beyond all endurance. I take my leave. No longer have I an interest in this house. (*Exits D.L.*)

MRS. TIFFANY. Get out, you *ow*dacious—you ruined woman! Never let me see your face again. Pack!

COUNT. Mrs. Tiffany—Madam—try to keep calm, control yourself. Let me help you, conduct you to the *silence* of your sitting room.

MRS. TIFFANY. (*Count takes her arm. She is dramatically exhausted*) Merci bow-coop.

COUNT. (*Helping her to the door*) You must rest. You

must relax. (*Aside*) And I must quick, be off with Seraphina. (*They exit D.L.*)

GERTRUDE. Mr. Trueman, I insist upon being heard. I claim it as a right!

TRUEMAN. Right! Ah, my girl you had more rights than you knew of, but you have forfeited them all. I'll start back to Catteraugus tomorrow. (*She starts toward him*) No. I have seen enough of what fashion can do! (*Exits D.L.*)

GERTRUDE. Oh, how heavy a penalty has my impudence cost me! Mr. Trueman's esteem—and that of Colonel Howard. I should be weeping, but pride has sealed my tears. I will go back to Geneva. Yes, but I must hurry and write them that I am coming. (*Sits at desk*) What shall I say? Lies I cannot tell. I will write—yes, I will write the truth. (*Writes*) I shall tell them how in trying to help, I was caught in my own web of innocence. Ah, what true pleasure there is in daring to be honest.

TRUEMAN. (*Enters D.L.*) There she is. If this girl's soul had only been as fair as her face—yet—she dared to speak the truth. I'll not forget that! A woman who refuses to tell a lie still has in her one spark of heaven. I will say goodby to her. Gertrude. What are you writing there?

GERTRUDE. I am writing the truth of what happened. The true facts to my friends in Geneva.

TRUEMAN. The true facts?

GERTRUDE. Yes. I have done nothing of which I am ashamed. Perhaps you desire to inspect my correspondence? There, read it if you like. (*Hands him the letter*)

TRUEMAN. So I will. (*Reads*) What's this? "French maid—the Count—an imposter!—disguised myself—to expose him." Thunder and lightning! I see it all. (*Aside*) Ah, she's a rare girl! Gertrude, I have found one true woman at last. And I will thrash every fellow that says a word against you! Now, my girl, one more truth. It is important that I knew if your heart is free or taken? Ah, you blush. There is a man. Who is he? Out with the truth! (*HOWARD enters D.L.*)

GERTRUDE. Colonel Howard here!

HOWARD. I have returned—
GERTRUDE. Yes?
HOWARD. I have returned with your book.
GERTRUDE. Thank you. (*Takes it*)
HOWARD. I have returned to bid you farewell. You, Gertrude, it is you who have exiled me. After your recent exposure—
TRUEMAN. What the plague have you got to say about exposure? And what have you to say to that little girl at all? The truth, man!
HOWARD. Very well, I will speak truthfully. I have long cherished a dream from which, in the past hour, I was rudely awakened.
TRUEMAN. Are you trying to say you suspect Gertrude there of—(*Angrily*)—of what no man shall ever suspect her of again while I'm above the ground! Well, I can tell you it was all a mistake. There, now the matter's settled. Go and ask her to forgive you.
GERTRUDE. Colonel Howard, if you will read this letter it will explain everything. (*Hands letter to Howard who reads*)
TRUEMAN. He don't deserve an explanation! Didn't I tell him that it was all a mistake? Refuse to beg your pardon. I'll teach him! I'll teach him! (*Raises stick*)
GERTRUDE. Pray, Mr. Trueman, desist for my sake.
HOWARD. Gertrude, how have I wronged you!
TRUEMAN. Oh, you'll beg her pardon now?
HOWARD. Her's Sir, and your's. Gertrude, I fear—
TRUEMAN. You needn't. She'll forgive you.
MRS. TIFFANY. (*Enters D.L., followed by MR. TIFFANY*) Mr. Tiffany, not another word. There is nothing more ungenteel than fretting over one's unpaid bills. Oh, what a *fa-tee-ging* day!
TRUEMAN. Ah, Antony, you are here just in time. I now can tell you and tell Gertrude why I came.
MRS. TIFFANY. (*To Gertrude*) You! Still in my house. You are dismissed—do you understand? Discharged!
TRUEMAN. Have you done, Madam? Then it's my turn. You remember, Antony, a blue-eyed, smiling girl—
MR. TIFFANY. Your daughter, Sir?
TRUEMAN. (*Remembers with emotion*) Yes, my only

daughter. Twenty years ago I found myself the richest farmer in Catteraugus. This cursed money made my girl an object of speculation. Every idle fellow came to court Ruth. There was one, who with his fine words and fair looks—ah, Ruth was taken with him. And one morning —the rascal robbed me of the only treasure I cherished —my daughter.

MR. TIFFANY. But you forgave her.

TRUEMAN. I did. The scroundrel thought he was marrying my gold, but he was mistaken. A year later, he forsook her! She came back to her old father. It couldn't last long—she pined—and pined—and—then— she died, and left a little girl. I swore that my unlucky wealth should never curse her, so I sent the child away, to be brought up by relatives in Geneva.

GERTRUDE. Geneva?

TRUEMAN. There she was taught true independence. She had hands—capacities—and learned to use them. For I resolved not to claim her until she'd found the man who was willing to take her for herself alone, not her money. Today I am going to claim her. There stands Ruth's child! Old Adam's heiress! Gertrude, Gertrude! My child! (*Gertrude rushes into his arms*)

MRS. TIFFANY. Gertrude! An heiress!

TRUEMAN. (*To Howard*) Step forward, young man. Gertrude is yours. Don't say a word. Don't bore me with your thanks. Well, Gertrude, and what do you say?

GERTRUDE. That I rejoice too much at having found a parent for my first act to be one of disobedience! Yes, he is the man. (*Gives her hand to Howard*)

HOWARD. Gertrude!

MILLINETTE. (*Enters D.L. with letter*) Madame! Madame! De letter! Mademoiselle Seraphina left de letter! A-dolph say he take de trunk. She going. She *gallop* avay vith de carriage.

MRS. TIFFANY. Letter? Gone away?

MR. TIFFANY. (*Snatches letter, reads*) "My dear Mama—when you receive this I shall be a countess! The Count and I were forced to be married privately..."

MRS. TIFFANY. (*Delighted*) Married?

MR. TIFFANY. (*In despair*) Married.

MILLINETTE. (*Horror-stricken*) Married! Oh, Madame, I vill tell everyting! Oh, dat *animal*! Dat *monstre*! He break my heart!
MRS. TIFFANY. Millinette, what are you saying?
MILLINETTE. Oh! He give de promise to marry me.
MRS. TIFFANY. The Count marry YOU!
MILLINETTE. *Oui*. But, Madame, de truth is dat he is not one Count, not at all! His name *a Paris* vas Gustave Tredmill. But he not one Frenchman at all, but he do live one long time *a Paris*. First he do live vid Monsieur Vermicelle—dere he vas de second cook.
MRS. TIFFANY. A cook?
MILLINETTE. Den he live vid *Monsieur* Tirenea, dere he was de head cook!
MRS. TIFFANY. A COOK!
MILLINETTE. *Voila*, now I tell de truth, Millinette feel one great deal better!
MRS. TIFFANY. Not a Count. What will everybody say? I shall faint!
SNOBSON. (*Enters, D.L., evidently a little intoxicated. Aside*) I won't stand for it. I say, Snobson, I won't stand for it. That extra mint julep has put the true puck in me. Mr. Tiffany, Sir, I'd like to know, Sir, why you assisted your daughter, Sir, in running away? I have been swindled, Sir.
MR. TIFFANY. (*Aside to Snobson*) Your salary shall be doubled—trebled—
SNOBSON. Nay, Sir! No more bribery, no more corruption.
TRUEMAN. Antony, silence that drunken jackass.
SNOBSON. This ain't your hash, Catteraugus, so keep your spoon out of the dish. I can knock him into a cocked hat with one single word. And now he's got my steam up—I will do it!
MR. TIFFANY. This is not the place—
SNOBSON. Place? Your place, Mr. Tiffany, Sir, is in the STATE'S PRISON! He's a FORGER! (*There is general confusion*: "Oh! What? No!") I said I'd expose him, and I have done it!
SERAPHINA. (*Enters D.L. in bonnet and shawl*) I hope

my note has not been discovered. (*Stops in surprise*) Oh! Everyone assembled!

MR. TIFFANY. (*To her and grabs her arm*) Tell me! Are—you—married?

SERAPHINA. Goodness, Papa, how you frightened me! No, I'm not married—quite.

MR. TIFFANY. Thank heaven.

MRS. TIFFANY. What has happened?

SERAPHINA. I came back for my jewels. The Count said a true Countess couldn't live without her jewels.

MR. TIFFANY. I may yet be saved! Seraphina, forget the Count. He is an imposter. And I beg you to marry— (*Aside*) Oh, heaven forgive me—to marry (*Points to Snobson*) HIM and save ME. And you, Mr. Trueman, if you will advance the money which I require, I can lift my head once again.

TRUEMAN. You—you have the cheek to ask me to aid you in becoming a greater villian than you are! Forgery! Selling your own daughter! Help you? Never!

GERTRUDE. Pray, Mr. Trueman—Grandfather, I should say—save him. I beg you.

TRUEMAN. Enough! I do not need your voice, child. I will settle this my way. (*To Snobson*) You! If I comprehend aright, you have been aware of, and a witness to, all his forgeries!

SNOBSON. You've hit the nail, Catteraugus!

TRUEMAN. You saw him forge the name?

SNOBSON. I did.

TRUEMAN. Repeatedly?

SNOBSON. Re-pea-ted-ly.

TRUEMAN. Then if he goes to the State's Prison, YOU'LL go, too. You are an accomplice, and ACCESSORY!

SNOBSON. (*Bewildered*) The deuce, so I am! I never thought of that! I must make myself scarce. I'll be off. Tif, I say Tif, that drunken old rip has got us in his power. Let's give him the slip and be off. They want men of genius in the West. You won't come, eh? Then I'm off without you. Goodby, Catteraugus! Which is the way to California? (*Exits D.L.*)

TRUEMAN. Antony, I'm not given to preaching, therefore I shall not say much about what you have done. Your face speaks for itself—the crime has brought its own punishment. And I will assist you financially, but upon one condition.

MR. TIFFANY. My friend, only name it.

TRUEMAN. You must sell your house and bundle your wife and daughter off to the country. There let them learn economy, true independence, instead of dependence upon a dressmaker; learn to live with home virtues, instead of foreign fashion.

MR. TIFFANY. My wife and daughter shall quit the city tomorrow.

MRS. TIFFANY. What!

MR. TIFFANY. We will go with you to Catteraugus!

TRUEMAN. Thunder and lightning, no! Keep clear of Catteraugus. I want none of your fashion there!

COUNT. (*Enters D.L.*) What can be detaining Seraphina? We must be off or all is lost.

MILLINETTE. (*Sees Count, rushes to him, holds him*) He is here! Ah, Gustave, *mon cher* Gustave! I have you now and ve never come apart no more.

TRUEMAN. Step forward, Mr. Count. And for the edification of fashionable society confess that you are an impostor.

COUNT. I? An impostor?

TRUEMAN. Your feminine friend has told us all about it.

MILLINETTE. I lost you. I re-find you. I tell all. I love you so!

TRUEMAN. Confess, and there may be help for you.

COUNT. Well, then I do confess I am no Count, but ladies and gentlemen, may I recommend myself as the best French cook, *ala mode de Paris*.

MRS. TIFFANY. Oh, Seraphina!

SERAPHINA. Oh, Mama!

TRUEMAN. If you promise to dress in your cook's attire and call upon all your fashionable acquaintances, I will set you up in business tomorrow. Better to turn stomachs than turn heads!

MILLINETTE. But you vill marry me?

COUNT. Give us your hand, Millinette! Madam, Mademoiselle, I hope you will pardon my conduct, but I heard in America, where you pay homage to titles, where FASHION makes the basest coin current, where you have no kings, no princes, no NOBILITY—

TRUEMAN. Stop! We have NOBILITY. We have kings, princes, and nobles in abundance—they are noble with the stamp of NATURE, not of FASHION. Yes, we have honest men, warm hearted and brave, and we have women—gentle, fair and true. I raise my stick and salute them. In America, good people do not need a title, for they ARE the finest of NOBILITY! (*Tableau. Music*)

GERTRUDE. (*Steps forward, addresses audience*).

But ere we end our play, a word with you—

HOWARD. (*He and each actor step forward, making a line for the epilogue*)

On honor say—Is our picture true?

MR. TIFFANY.

Fashion drove me close to a prison wall.

TRUEMAN.

Fashion made hypocrites of you all.

MRS. TIFFANY.

I've been deceived. Fashion, I thought was vital.

SERAPHINA.

Fashion lost me both a husband and a title.

COUNT.

A Count no more, I'm no more account.

TRUEMAN.

But to a nobler title you may mount,
And be in time—who knows?—an honest man.

MILLINETTE.

Oh, *oui*, my *adorable hero*, I know you can.

SNOBSON. (*Enters D.L. and stands in line*)

I aspired to rise, a fashionable gent to be,
But, damn it, fashion didn't take up me.

GERTRUDE.

Thus our play has shown in its ruling passion,
And portrayed, we hope, the tensil value—of Fashion.

CURTAIN

OTHER TITLES AVAILABLE FROM BAKER'S PLAYS

CANDIDA

George Bernard Shaw
Adapted and abridged by Aurand Harris

Comedy / 3m, 2f/ Interior

Probably Shaw's most popular play, *Candida* recounts the love sickness of young poet Eugene Marchbanks for Candida, wife of the Rev. Morell. At first, Morell is amused; but when he begins to doubt his wife's love, he becomes disturbed and angered. The poet becomes the stronger suitor, Morell realizes his weaknesses and Candida, one of the most remarkable women in dramatic literature, gives strength to her husband and teaches Marchbanks how to love. Harris offers a superb adaptation for competition, for study, and for introduction to one of the classics of modern theatre.

BAKERSPLAYS.COM

OTHER TITLES AVAILABLE FROM BAKER'S PLAYS

BREAKING UP IS HARD TO DO

Dennis Snee

Comedy / 4m, 3f, Extras / Open Stage

Jonathan and Margaret have enjoyed (endured) a marriage of fifty years and a day, when we join them for their rocking chair confrontation over past battles and future prospects. Bob and Doris, in their 30's, have been more or less going steady when Bob announces a job transfer that will take him—and his mother—to Arizona. Marshall and Carolyn are a high school senior and junior respectively, who have been formal steadies for three months. Marshall's delusions of male grandeur give rise to his humorous but unwarranted reservations about breaking poor Carolyn's heart by asking for his ring back. The Narrator blends these vignettes as he sets props and offers his wisdom on the human conditions in this wonderfully funny and believable play about the one aspect of the human folly: love.

BAKERSPLAYS.COM

OTHER TITLES AVAILABLE FROM BAKER'S PLAYS

ALICE IN AMERICA-LAND
or *Through the Picture Tube and What Alice Found There*

Dennis Snee

Comedy Fantasy / Flexible / Open Stage with Backdrops

In this fresh and lively update of Lewis Carroll's classic, Alice takes a journey through the picture tube of her family's television, and meets a mad collection of characters — with a certain difference! A White Rabbit — who lives in fear of someone's dropping "the big one." A Mock Turtle — who's a champion of consumer rights. A Dodo who's a guitarist, a Dormouse seeking political office and an Eagle who lives in the past. The Duke and Duchess have switched life roles — she's a "working duchess" while he's a "house duke." Alice herself becomes the unwitting subject for a showbiz roast with two aging, bitter comedians — the Mad Hatter and the March Hare. Through it all, Alice just wants to return home to her beloved cat. Just when it seems as though this mad world of America-land will drive her as mad as the inhabitants, she awakens, safe at home, her cat in her lap. A fanciful, biting, always funny tale of a contemporary Alice that will delight all audiences.

BAKERSPLAYS.COM